At The Fun Park

Dawn McMillan

At the fun park,
we go up.

At the fun park,
we go down.

At the fun park,
we go up and down.

At the fun park,
we go round.

At the fun park,
we go round and round.

At the fun park,
we go bump.

At the fun park, we have ice-cream!